A Grammar for Snow

Richard Luftig

A GRAMMAR FOR SNOW
Copyright©2019 Richard Luftig
All Rights Reserved
Published by Unsolicited Press
Printed in the United States of America.
First Edition July 2019.

All rights reserved. Printed in the United States of America. No part of this book may be used or reproduced in any manner whatsoever without written permission except in the case of brief quotations embodied in critical articles or reviews.

Attention schools and businesses: for discounted copies on large orders, please contact the publisher directly.

For information contact:
Unsolicited Press
Portland, Oregon
www.unsolicitedpress.com
orders@unsolicitedpress.com
619-354-8005

Cover Design: Kathryn Gerhardt
Editor: S.R. Stewart

ISBN: 978-1-947021-95-2

For Diane, my wife, and my children Amy and David.

Acknowledgements

"Compromise County" appeared in *Rootstalk*.

"Along the Ohio" appeared in *Rootstalk*.

"Galois Theory" appeared in *Rockvale Journal*.

"Agnes at One-Hundred" appeared in *Sierra Nevada College Review*.

"The Point" appeared in *Emry's Journal*.

"A Note to My Unemployment Counselor" appeared in *California Quarterly*.

"Snow Talk" appeared in *Visions International*.

"One Million" appeared in *Conch River Review* and in England *Obsessed with Pipework*.

"Wild Plums Along an Idaho Road" appeared in *Avocet*.

"A Grammar for Snow" appeared in *Broadkill Review*.

"Four Kinds of Writing Paper" appeared in *Lummox Journal* and in Hong Kong in *Cha*.

"West River" appeared in *The Glass Cherry*.

"The Old Couple" appeared in *Four Quarters*.

"Night Along the Susquehanna" appeared in *Pegasus*.

"Irrational Numbers" appeared in Canada in *Queen's Quarterly*.

"Passacaglia" appeared in *Third Wednesday*.

"Speeding Through Kansas" appeared in *Westview*.

"George Washington's Bridge" appeared in *Blue Unicorn* and in Canada in *Challenger*.

"Drought" appeared in *The Write Place at the Write Time* and in India in *Wagon*.

"The Last Clothesline in South Dakota" appeared in *Pegasus*.

"Returning to Illinois" appeared in *Ilya's Honey*.

"Senior Center" appeared in *Ilya's Honey*.

"Talking to Van Gogh at Three a.m. outside Kellogg, Iowa" appeared in *Homestead Review*.

"Yard Sale" appeared in *Natural Bridge*.

"Conjugations" appeared in *Plainsongs* and in Canada in *Whetstone*.

"Current" appeared in *Literary Yard*.

"Runaway Truck Lane" appeared in *West Ward Quarterly*.

"Lake, Night, Minnesota" appeared in *Old Northwest Review*.

"Solstice" appeared in *Piedmont Journal of Poetry and Fiction*.

"The Old Ladder" appeared in *Oasis*.

"Kadoka" appeared in *Wisconsin Review*.

"Buddhist Ink and Brush" appeared in *Suisson Valley Review*.

"Early Bird Special" appeared in *Straylight Magazine*.

"Ode to Bacon" appeared in *Homestead Review*.

"It is Good" appeared in *The Griffin*.

"And Another Thing" appeared in *Rockhurst Review*.

"What They Had" appeared in *Third Wheel*.

"First Signs of Spring" appeared in *Badlands Literary Journal*.

"While I Wasn't Looking" appeared in *Birmingham Arts Journal*.

"How to Write a Poem in a Café" appeared in *Evening Street Review*.

"Love Letter" appeared in *Harpur Palate*.

"The Woman in Hospice Dreams of Paris" appeared in *Iodine Poetry Review*.

"Waiting for the Parade" appeared in *"Front Porch Review*.

"Cornflowers" appeared in *South Dakota Review*.

"Local Branch" appeared in *Off the Coast*.

"Teleology" appeared in *Poet's Pen* and in England in *Obsessed with Pipework*.

"Off the Map" appeared in *Potomac Review*.

"Still Life" appeared in *Common Ground Review* and in Australia in *Speedpoets*.

"Somewhere Over Pennsylvania" appeared in *Roanoke Review*.

"Mall Walking" appeared in *George Washington Review*.

"Open House" appeared in *Buffalo Bones* and in Australia in *Redoubt*.

"So, This is Karaoke" appeared in *Sidewalk*.

"Speed Dating" appeared in *Willard & Maple*.

"The Safest Town in Indiana" appeared in *Hard Road to Hoe*.

"The Palm Reader is Packing it in" appeared in *Broome Review*.

"Ancestor Trees" appeared in *Owen Wister Review*.

"Fly Over States" appeared in *Red Wheelbarrow*.

"Pruning a Limb" appeared in *Poetic Eloquence*.

"Bolero Silencio" appeared in *Mother Earth International* and in England in *Gentle Reader*.

"My Second Annual Farewell Poem" appeared in *West Ward Quarterly*.

Poems

Compromise County, Illinois	15
Old Car Parade	17
Along the Ohio	19
Galois Theory	21
Agnes at One-Hundred	23
The Point	24
A Note to My Unemployment Insurance Counselor	25
Snow Talk	27
One Million	29
Wild Plums Along an Idaho Road	30
A Grammar for Snow	32
West River	34
The Four Kinds of Writing Paper	36
The Old Couple	38
Along the Susquehanna	40
Irrational Numbers	42
Passacaglia	44
Speeding Through Kansas	47
George Washington's Bridge	49
Drought	50
The Last Clothesline in South Dakota	51
Returning to Illinois	52

Senior Center	54
Speaking with Van Gogh at Three a.m. Outside Kellogg, Iowa	55
Conjugations	57
Current	58
Runaway Truck Lane	59
Solstice	61
An Old Ladder	63
Kadoka	64
Buddhist Ink and Brush	66
Early Bird Special	68
Ode to Bacon	69
It Is good	71
An Old Rocker Comes Up at Auction	73
And Another Thing	75
What they had	77
First Signs of Spring	78
How to Write a Poem in a Cafe	79
Love Letter	81
The Woman in Hospice Remembers Paris	83
Waiting for the Parade	84
Cornflowers	86
Local Branch	87
Teleology	88
Off the Map	89
Still Life	90

Somewhere Over Pennsylvania	91
Mall Walking	93
Open House	94
So, This is Karaoke	95
Speed Dating	97
The Safest Town in Indiana	98
The Palm Reader is Packing It In	99
Ancestor Trees	101
Fly Over States	102
Pruning a Limb	104
Bolero Silencio	105
My Second Annual Farewell Poem	106

A Grammar for Snow

Compromise County, Illinois

The people who came here settled
on a life, on a land so flat that one
might get lost on a turn-around
plat of single farm. First,

crops: corn, winter wheat, beans
that decorated acreage like dots
in a Seurat painting. Later,
saplings of windbreak trees,

spruce, sycamore, the occasional
cottonwood, twisted and gnarled
like the trunks of the old, German
men who planted them, watched

them grow even as they shrunk
and shriveled. Men who still
arose at dawn to work this land
long after their best time was done.

Now, one-hundred, two-hundred
years and acres later, the grief
of failed crops, land, luck, love,
stick like the gumbo of April

mud and their grandsons of grandsons
have left, selling what they could,

giving away the rest of whatever
wasn't foreclosed or signed away.

And they, lifted away like topsoil
in an endless, prairie wind,
moving up, moving out
to cities where they never want

it to grow cold, grow wet.
Where they would live their lives
without even a single, hard freeze
if they could, leaving behind

the stubborn ghosts
of those first farmers who
took their best chances, now
making do with sandstone

tombstones, the names, dates,
lives worn away. Now guarded
hard by what's left of withered
trees, their weary branches fighting

January winds, so strong they blow
sheets of freezing snow sideways,
trying hard not to give in again
to what they might have been.

Old Car Parade

First, comes the '51 Studebaker,
the one pointed like a rocket,
then the two-toned Desoto Firelite
with its backwings curved
like a hawk catching an updraft.
Later, the '50 Nash, so squat
that the top half of the white walls

are obscured. And the drivers:
all with short sleeves, sporting
ball caps with names of retired
battleships across the bills,
their gray-haired, tanned forearms
resting on the sill of the rolled-down
windows. Last, the '42 Packard

driven by an old man wearing
a long-sleeved dress shirt,
tie, and fedora worn smooth
from everyday use, steering
with one hand and lightly tapping
the chrome side mirror like he is playing
some old Perry Como love song

only he can hear. He remembers
how he would lean hard out of the turns
or in toward the girl, now his wife,

sitting next to him, waving and tossing candy
to the crowd, and those days when
he would kiss her and kiss her
and she could think of nothing but him.

Along the Ohio

This river with so many meanders,
and oxbows that at times it seems
like it has no idea which way
to flow. And the towns

that run along; confused,
without direction as if
folks believe that if
the damn water would just

straighten itself out, run
pure and plumb, folks
might see what they need
to save the place, keep

things ahead of the curve.
But here, at Coropolis, Crown City,
Maysville and Martin's Ferry,
the deserted, boarded-up stores

show their rears to the river
and the banks seem to have lost
any interest in watching water pass
downstream. The only occupants

left are bald tires,
rusting oil drums,

broken quart bottles of High Life
and the occasional sofa

dumped when people thought
no one looking. Even the houses
seem to have given up
the ghost: back yards

scattered with driftwood
and weeds, save for one
with an ornament of a fat,
old, Dutch woman bending

over her tulips, bloomers
mooning the water and a family
of plastic ducks wondering
when it will be their turn to leave.

Galois Theory

*That which makes the connection between two sets of
phenomena easier to understand.*

The way we struggle
to explain this life,

how one senses
a future for newborn

grass while it sleeps
beneath a foot of February

snow. Or lotus stars
bursting upon frosted window

panes. No, whatever equation
we seek must contain

that push and pull
of equilibrium,

always taking into
account the gravity

of our situation;
this fulcrum,

that hovers
between points

that live in delicate
balance, demanding

whatever is done
to one half of us

must also occur
with the other.

Agnes at One-Hundred

I always thought that I would grow
into my mother's face.
I wanted to see how God
intended me to look,
more out of curiosity
than anything else. I hope
He appreciates the joke.

I can remember my mother
warning me that I was plain,
not nearly pretty enough
to attract a man and maybe
she was right but look-
there's something to be said
for homeliness. It's a damn sight
easier to maintain than beauty.
Lasts a lot longer too.

In the end, gravity always wins.

It's not that I'm afraid of death—
more like I'm not all that interested
one way or the other.
I've simply learned that age rests
on one's shoulder like a quiet bird,
not tame but not exactly timid either.

The Point

Let's start by giving him a name.
Harry or Lance or even Ira will do.
I mean, the point is who wants to go through life
known as A or B or some other letter
of the alphabet? Just being A is enough
to make him forget who he is
and never knowing where he came from,
he freezes into a simple dot, his life atrophied
like a paralyzed limb. He drops
roots, watching helplessly as lines and vectors
and angles shoot out, venturing from their point
of departure like ungrateful children embarking
on adventures, leaving the Old Man behind.
He could not go even if he wanted, the moment
he moved he would no longer be the same,
no longer be A, as if crossing the street
or even stretching his legs would turn
Harry into Lance. So, he stays put, afraid,
and collapsing under the weight
of his own gravity, curls into a ball
dreaming of a heaven where he will finally
be able to repent, defy gravity and go straight.

A Note to My Unemployment Insurance Counselor

I am sending you this email
that you can read each Monday
instead of my appearing every week.
I thought it would save us both trouble.

To use your phrase, I have
been actively looking for work.
Nightly, I talk to the bar-keep
over at Jack's Grill to see if

he knows of anything, and just
the other day I wrote Bill Gates
with some improvements he
could make if he just hired me.

Down at Rebecca's Café,
I regularly read the want ads
from old copies of the weekly
Pennysaver but there seems

to be precious few openings
for brain surgeon. However,
I am happy to report
that I am making progress

with the beautiful red-haired
woman with the sweet scent
of strawberry shampoo
who sits every day at the table

next to mine and eats a pecan
muffin, drinks herbal tea
and reads letters from a past
lover. I am getting close

to asking her to join me
at my regular table, and I
will report each week
with details as they occur.

Snow Talk

Crows chatter gossip on telephone lines.
They call long distance to anyone
who has not yet heard the news.
The first blizzard of the season is on its way.
It is like this every year when late

November decides it's had enough
and is ready to give up to the bully
who lives just the next month over.
So, it makes its final exit at just
the moment you would least expect.

In town, talk of accumulations, school closings,
whether the graveyard shift of the paper mill
will let out early has become the drift
of every conversation. Down at the café,
men stir their coffee and memories

of big ones that took place decades
ago, add inches with each retelling
until it is a wonder that the stuff
ever melted at all. And then it comes;
stopping all conversation in its tracks.

First, in a flurry of slowness, flakes turn
somersaults in windless air, then heavy,
out of breath, but still, without a sound.

An inch, two inches an hour until, stopping
traffic, if there ever was any, it leaves

every town in the county to fend for itself.
It is an artist that gives hats to cars, beards
to parking meters: even barbed-wire
seems to have a sense of humor. And on
the Main Street that cuts through town,

empty, silent, save for the soft,
muffled grind of a sand truck,
it gives the vacant, boarded- up
stores, one beautiful excuse, if just
for today, why folks aren't here.

One Million

I asked the cashier down at the café today
for the one-millionth customer discount.
She laughed a bit, said she liked the idea.
We'll start right now, and you'll be number one.

My wife got on me for swearing up a storm.
Said she'd been counting the last thirty years
and I had taken the Lord's name in vain
a million times. Jesus, that can't be right.

Stopped and looked out at the near frozen fields,
at birds fighting the high-hawk winds.
They're flying off for the winter, leaving me
to ask for the millionth time why I am still here.

Wild Plums Along an Idaho Road

This tree-sagging bounty
so ripe for the picking,
their show-off, amethyst
cluster just before fall.

You, the survivors
of sunscald and frost,
bindweed and chokecherry
that wanted nothing less

than to cut you off
from cool April rains.
But look how you have
stood to survive it all

and lived to share first
fruits for whoever like me
might randomly pass along.
And I who have spent

my years like a handful
of change. If only I could
learn how you do it,
how you call home

wherever you've been
sown, I would be content

to make do with whatever
is left of these threadbare

dreams; hold full to this world,
crown, root and core, live
out the remains of my life
one sweet season at a time.

A Grammar for Snow

I who have yearned a lifetime
to learn their names
like a discoverer in a foreign land.

Blizzard and squall, band
flurries, grains of graupel
in soft hail or pellets.

Plants also: Snow pea,
snow belle and poppy.
Snowdrops, bowing

in sweet pairs like necks
of white cranes. Blossoms
that poke through frost

on a March day when
no one is looking
and then break your heart

when false-spring
recants on its promise
like early love that swore

to be faithful forever.
Watermelon snow; pink
then red. Blood snow,

they call it in the Sierra.
A snow that lingers, holds
on, winter to winter,

year after year, longer
than we thought we
ever would, when

first we learned
the correct syntax,
and now struggling

to keep our own special
order like that winter
when we began to love.

West River

Although some have remained,
most have moved, far from West River,
back East to the Dakota that lies
off the Missouri. East to land black
with furrows or thick with wheat.
Land so flat it slices off angles at horizon.

Further East to Mitchell, Yankton,
Elkton, South Shore. Where houses sit
on tracts cheek-to -jowl; quarter
sections reduced to nickel sized
gardens filled with snap peas
and rhubarb, marigold and memory.

People sit on porches or in parlors
with upright pianos and rockers covered
with comforters. They close their eyes,
yearn to remember what it is like
tonight in West River. West where bluffs
keep watch on the Missouri, west

past Murdo where the earth knobbed
with bumps and freckles and sunspots
burns to August brown. Where grass,
sparse and starved, gasps
for water, yielding to constant
wind; sometimes a whisper,

often a muffled sob, but then hissing
hard threats when it learns that it is not
the center of attention. Raising Cain,
raising dust, this land spewing
itself, propagating. Dust begetting
dust, until it becomes reborn

as yellow grit air. Much later,
that night, a lifetime from now,
West River people will lie
beneath a cold, white moon,
tucked away in skeletons
that used to be towns, dead

places like the light
years that grow between stars.
They will hold their breath
and listen East, trying to recall
a place where rain touches skin,
falling thick with gardens and wheat.

The Four Kinds of Writing Paper

From the Chinese

I. Wild Geese

Swallows, willows, sparrows, spruce.
Wild geese scattered among white pine.
Flying and migratory,
like children coming home
to visits aging parents.
Transitory guests in the house.

II. Blue Cloud

Wisteria in clear wind.
A sky speckled in sunlight.
It is the clouds' turn to talk.
The moon stands respectfully
waiting to search sleeping stars
for its genealogy

III. Cicada Wing

Who would have guessed seventeen
years, the time to be reborn?
Old age now measured in days.
Death arriving in a month.
Better to never see offspring

than to watch them grow old alone.

IV. Six Times Lucky

How lucky and difficult
to complete anything in life.
Still, gardens move to the edge
of hayfields, solitary
bees bustle among flowers
searching for their communion.

The Old Couple

The old couple down the road
do not tan in the August
sun. Instead, they stroke
the napes of cats curled in circles

in their laps in shaded lawn
chair rockers that swing their legs
in arcs of long, long dance.
In morning, they follow the shade

around the yard like sundials,
heat tugging at their heels,
until afternoon forces their backs
again against the bricks. At three,

they move inside to count time
by naps and soaps and yesterdays
leftover meals. Sometimes, if
the morning is cool they weed

flowers in a clandestine
garden with spades and trowels
that well-meaning children
have forbidden them to use.

If visitors call, they sit
in the parlor, happy to haul

out shoe boxes weighted
with letters and photos foxed

and cracked at the edges.
Later, the threat of night
encircles the house as they bask
in the flickering light of a kitchen TV.

At nine, they go to the heart
of the house, checking locks
and pulses and laying their day
by the night stand with her

glasses and his hearing aid.
One will need to hear for two
while two will dream as one
alone. They sleep like flowers

closed for the night
until morning comes.
Then, lingering in bed, long
as they might, they grip

the hollow of the day,
donning familiar eyes
and ears and warming
fresh milk to feed the cats.

Along the Susquehanna

1.
The moon persists
In making its faces;
Taunting the dark water
Along an ice-locked shore.

Up in some bony branch
Of a wizened sycamore, an owl,
No, perhaps a loon, is telling
Tall tales it knows nothing

About. This night is so
Young, the season so advanced.
Clouds exist only to hide
An indiscretion of sky.

2.
Each step might as well
Be a thought; old dreams

That circle back on itself.
I heard once that cypress

Can thrust and pull,
Lift and drop when no one

Is near enough to tell
Their story once removed.

3.
Even in May, the moon
      Cannot burn off dew;
Clouds will not light up stars.

Each knows its role:
      Like the soft
Lacing of a glove.

I stand alone; a sentry
      Pine, searching the wind
For its hidden thoughts.

Irrational Numbers

A number that cannot be expressed as a simple fraction. If it were a decimal, it would go on forever.

I wouldn't much trust any
of them with something
important like buying
a car or choosing the best

college. Hell, they
don't even know
enough to end in a neat
point or round themselves

off against the hard edges
of their everyday lives.
No, maybe not. But still
they manage to carry

on, survive, keep
moving forward
(or is it back) forever,
year after year,

an endless line,
never repeating.
Eternal optimists
with no regrets.

Like us that day
we became one,
put down roots,
solid and square,

seeking the common
denominator to lives
we thought would
be as easy as pi.

Passacaglia

A slow, funereal piece, composed with a steady, unchanging left hand

This ground bass
is losing time
like the clock
        on the mantle

he has wound
        each mourning
        for her: trying,
just barely,

        to keep some hope
alive. Bach knew
all of this:
        how each Sarabande,

that saddest
        of dances,
        depends on
keeping the hands

        apart, the left
like heartbeats
in dead of winter
        that throb

to stave off loss,
>
while the right
>
absorbed, in
in its own

>
blizzard
of keys,
races away,
>
not caring

any longer
>
about the other
>
octaves
of this world.

It is like
>
the canon
>
she would play
in C major,

>
that brightest
of keys,
but now
>
consigned

to a minor
>
universe
>
that echos
a round,

>   but with one
> voice gone,
> or a partita
>   once perfect,
>
>   now empty
> with the absence
> of a first
>   violin.

Speeding Through Kansas

These semis
are prairie
schooners:
sailing west,
speeding past
cornfields, barns,
frontage roads,
scatters
of windbreak
trees. And the towns:

all *video-land*
second-hand
stores turned
hand-to-mouth,
brick-to-dust,
falling in,
fading fast.
They hold out
false fronts,
false hopes

and even now
can't admit
how anything
sown into
this wind-blown,

silt-loam
land could
ever be
destined
to survive.

George Washington's Bridge

was made of ivory and steel,
not the wood that Gilbert Stuart thought
to paint in his portrait with those sunken
cheeks and sour face that made him
look as if he had swallowed a perch.

His dentist's nightmare, that bridge
and plate rotten and corroded by years
of Hollandaise sauce and lemon juice,
a nasty habit picked up in France
from too many gout-filled Christmas

feasts at court. If only George had known
of chrome, his countenance improved
on every schoolhouse wall for generations,
for as dental science had come to learn;
there is no plate like chrome for the Hollandaise.

Drought

Out in the back of farms,
dead, rusted tractors wait,
impatient for a winter bath.

It has been dry here so long
that even ducks have forgotten
how to tilt back their heads

and drink from the skies.
Little is left that is not
ash-gray dirt: just dust,

cross-hatched with tracks
of long-gone sparrows,
and these parched, fallow

fields that are left to eke
out a life on their own.
They sit; scarred, seed-

to-sedge. Sand-blasted,
erased, year-in, year-out,
like some ignored spinster,

who wants, waits, wishes
for more but is always
too afraid to ask.

The Last Clothesline in South Dakota

The people here must have been in a hurry,
leaving the stained, stuffed sofa on the front porch,
now a haven for field mice. Inside, a dresser,
its chest puffed out, two right women's mud- boots,
a headless doll, red toy truck missing two wheels,
all strewn across the living-room floor. What's left

of the windows blown out for target practice,
gape open to winter fields long left to seed.
And in the side yard, next to a broken swing,
rusted slide, tether-pole with the leather ball missing,
a thin rope still runs between two splintered
trees, clothespins stand guard like sentry soldiers,

and further down the line, next to the wrens
hanging on by their toes, swaying back
and forth like trapeze artists practicing
to stay aloft above dozens of broken beer bottles
that serve for their net, a child's blanket, sheets
begging to be borne again by the icy, northern wind.

Returning to Illinois

This place where plats are square
and homes sit a mile apart as if
to avoid prying ears of folks who swear
they don't repeat gossip so they're

only going to say this once.
Where trees were planted generations ago
as windbreaks for thirty mile-an-hour
winds that people refer to as a breeze,

but whatever you want to call it
bites hard in March, picking up
dirt and grit from fallow fields
to deposit in snow banks

that grow each day without gaining
much interest from folks
who've been watching this play out
longer than they want to recall.

I need to return to diners where sausage
is a food group and people die of ham.
Where meatloaf, mashed potatoes,
gravy, creamed corn all touch on the plate

and everything lies as flat as this land
instead of at a forty-five-degree angle

decorated with a sprig of parsley.
Where the waitress calls me *darlin'*

twice within one minute of my arrival,
where Rotary meets the third Thursday
of the month and the vegetarian specials,
tossed and green bean salad, are loaded

with bacon bits. This place where
there are exactly five Democrats
in the county and three of them are
having breakfast at the table across from mine,

wearing seed caps, down vests,
chortling over whatever the guy
with the oxygen tank is reading
from his cellphone, all the while

eating their biscuits and gravy
so thick that you can twirl it on
your fork, coffee as black as the earth
that the tractors are plowing in the fields.

Senior Center

We return day after day like migratory doves
to newspapers, books, the blue light of CNN
with the mute on. No, the local news is more important—
a friend's scheduled surgery, another remarrying
at age 83 to a babe ten years younger than himself.

Coffee and donuts, twenty-five cents each
from the bakery uptown, sprinkled with jokes
we've told dozens of times before.

Lunch; turkey a-la-king, Friday fish
for Catholics who swear they've never heard
of Vatican II. And the seating: always unreserved
which we've nevertheless been reserving for years.

Then the tables cleared for our games of canasta
that have gone on longer than forever: four-handed
if you don't count the folks commenting on each trick,
none of us ever trying for trump but rather
content to simply lay down our hearts.

Speaking with Van Gogh at Three a.m. Outside Kellogg, Iowa

I ask if I might give him a few pointers
about how stars really don't rotate
in penumbras of color, or how his room
in Arles has such tilted perspective
that if he actually laid down on that bed
he would roll off and end up in the middle
of the floor. He says he is all ears

on the subject but I don't think
he is paying attention. He reports
that when he paints, he remains
of two minds like those brushstrokes
that fly off in all directions, or knife-palette
trees that twist at the end of the fields.

I ask how he manages to get
his mulberry trees to explode
into diamonds. He smiles,
shrugs, says it is like how
corn manages to grow
straight in rows, arms flung,

and joyfully touches the shoulders
of its neighbors in midnight
communion. Or how gyroscopes
circle in separate orbits realize

without fully knowing how
moonlight basks farmhouses
set miles apart, each trying to make
sense of their own spinning worlds.

Conjugations

Living without you teaches one to forget
the reflexive pronoun. There can be no *self*
when there is only air to compare *me*
with, when what remains of *we*
is the one of us missing each
morning as I pass by the half-mirror

in the silent hall. In Spanish,
it is possible to change *disappear*
from verb to noun. Translating
the word into English yields a place
where we have been, where I am
condemned to remain invisible.

Current

A river needs descent of an eighth of an inch per mile to produce a flow, and if that is the case, our river probably fails—Henry David Thoreau

This river has nowhere special
to go and all the time to do it.
Now it is late autumn and still
it struggles to move, shake itself

loose, get its dead logs
downstream before the first
grips of winter grab hard
upon the land. And we

too stuck in this drive-by
town, this fly-over State,
need to keep current,
collect the twigs and branches

of rumors, kindling really,
for the best gossip that allows
us to stoke the fires
of our February lives.

Runaway Truck Lane

Sign found on the Interstate

They may have run off when the moon was down
and no one was looking. Or maybe they broke out
from a darkened lot in Maine or Kansas, a stockyard
near Cheyenne, an oil refinery outside Shreveport,
figuring that they wouldn't be missed until morning.

But now they're on the lam, fleeing along
the Interstate, halfway into their getaway to some
distant coast or central plain, moving mostly late
at night as if they might be recognized
from their pictures on a milk carton.

The names on their grills--Peterbilt, Mack,
Western Star and Crane-- are splashed
with mud and bugs to keep them incognito,
their tires humming in the right lane, bodies heavy
with distant bills of lading, or deadheading

to Texas, trying all the while to avoid
the weigh scales and troopers who would like
nothing better than to write them up, send in
reports as to their whereabouts. But it is just
before dawn that they love the most,

coming down over the mountains, singing
with hot blasts of abandon through their exhausts,
accelerating downhill, faster and faster still,
then reluctantly shifting to lower gears
but anxious all the while to avoid those uphill

ramps so determined to trap them in a clinch
of sand straight up to the hubs of each axle,
taking the tires into unwanted custody
until a posse of tow trucks can arrive,
sinking in their claws to drag them home.

Solstice

He thinks the best way
to deal with winter

is simply by staying
alive. It is the same

as how he puts up
with every day

loss; water a plant,
feed the distant cat.

His life now a play
that people no longer

attend; much like
how the angled

light gets short
shrift this shortest

day of the year.
But still he will

follow the walkway
down to the bottom,

of the drive, check
the empty mailbox

that on the best of days
might be stuffed with circulars

that could fill at least part
of his afternoon, the black

ice an overcoat he would
just as soon slip on.

An Old Ladder

Twenty feet long, lying in the weeds.
Shedding its skin in splinters from the years.
Each of its step-grids yield a hopscotch
for rabbits, a needed plat for slugs
to explore silted treasures below.

Bend down close, get to eye level.
See its perspective like a vanishing point
of a spur-line railroad track that once
led to some silo or barn or factory,
long torn up, torn down, dreams

that people who lived here must have
dreamed of but which never came to pass.
And still, this ancient wood hangs on, each
rung pressed to the chest of this rich, flat earth,
waiting, no, yearning, to prop up a life again.

Kadoka

In Kadoka, South Dakota,
the main business of town is dying.
The worn-out, flat-front, sand-stone
stores huddle and shield their faces
from a constant, grinding wind.

The town lists to railroads,
it's back pressed flush to rusting
tracks, waiting for trains that won't
come anymore. Out from
Kadoka, the ribbon roads

crease black and empty fields,
land so flat you can drop a line
and weight and come up plumb
crazy from the straightness of it all.
Those roads run east to the end

of town where buildings straggle
and fade into fence posts and winter
wheat. Or west, past where the town
used to be, out to the highway lined
with truck stops full of placemat ads

for Yogi Bear Campgrounds and Badland Motels.
The graduating class, this year just twelve,
drive dusty brown beaters or trucks tuned

to the country station in Pierre, heading
to Denver or Cheyenne, or wherever

there's work. Old people sit and watch
the blacktop roads buckle and roll
against August. They count time
by quarter hours and moons and wait
for cars passing through to anywhere

but here.

Buddhist Ink and Brush

From afar boulders
Become alabaster.

Racks of clouds
Rippled, rounded,

Pines hunched
Bundled in frost.

Here rice paper
Stars are miracles

Dropped from
The moon.

This landscape
Where we breathe,

Rest, breathe
Again: place

Of vanishing
Point, of outcomes

Not taken
That fall away

At the edges
Of negative space.

Early Bird Special

I'll have the open-faced,
turkey sandwich with gravy
and an extra plate. We'll share.
And Budweiser. If you could bring us
an empty glass that would be nice.

Afterwards, they will return
to the home they've shared
for the last fifty years: she, driving,
he, giving directions and telling
her again about the first time they met.

Ode to Bacon

You, the most regal of meats,
cured with the sweet essence
of trees: Hickory, Sugar Maple,
Applewood, all with enough salt
to preserve a mariner's food supply
on a voyage to the New World.

Made with love by pigs
in a blanket of grease,
best wrapped and deep-fried
with Twinkies and corn dogs
at county fairs. The only thing
that makes lettuce and tomato

edible if I must consume
my vegetables. I, who choose
you four times in the Pick-Five
breakfast at my local diner,
who put you in a blender
for my health shake, who order

you *ala mode* with apple pie.
The only true impediment I see
to a conversion to Judaism.
No, *never*, I say to the report
that people who abstain live two years
longer than those who eat you.

No, never to
two more
Long
Agonizing,
Baconless
Years.

it is good

to listen in summer
for the screen door
that shuts with a bang-
-and-a quarter when
it takes its bounce,

and in autumn
when you pause
on the front steps
and the wind brings
the first, fallen
leaves to your face.

In winter, it is good
to stay inside and hear
scrape of snow shovel
on walkway, or water
boiling on the stove
for soup, the air filled
with spiced remembrances
like a returning friend.

But it is best in those first,
unsure mornings of spring
when mockingbirds try out
their newest songs while
we lie side- by- side,

breath- to- breath, recalling
how we were young, so
full of passion, that our
hearts wept for the world.

An Old Rocker Comes Up at Auction

She used it to coax fussy children
back to sleep in the August dark,
or figure out how to mend a marriage
going bad in the next bedroom over.

Through those trying nights,
he prayed in it over how to pay
the bills before the bank foreclosed
on what was left of this house,

this land. This old chair saw it all.
These runners cut from cherry

on the downstairs, fireplace mantel.
wood by someone her grandfather
must have known, the dowels shaped

by hand to fit snug like the family
photographs placed cheek-to-jowl
They say that the arms are always

the first to show its age and these
are worn smooth with worry,
pocked-marked by cigarette burns
when he would nod off to reruns

on late night TV, forgetting
to flick the ashes, stub out
the butts, and then be jolted
awake by the crick in his neck.

And she, never quite dreaming
how their lives might be assigned
a lot number to be shouted out,
offered up, to the highest bidder.

And Another Thing

You and I are probably not reincarnations
of William the Conqueror nor great
descendants of Joan of Arc. Things
are funny that way. Why is it we

were not Ignatz Stromonkowski,
in a prior life, some guy who made
pig-liver sandwiches for the Emperor
outside Warsaw during the Middle Ages

or not a disembodied tribal king
who became the number one gene donor
for the European continent but instead merely
lunch for a lion on the savannah plain?

And another thing: everything we write
in our diary or journal will not
be fascinating grist for neo-
deconstructionist-revisionist reviewers

trying to make sense of our indelible
literary symbolism. No, the best we can
probably hope for is that somebody
will find Volume One of Two-Hundred

of our stuff in some attic years after we die,
thumb through the first three pages

and murmur approvingly that at least
we used the correct usage of *lie* and *lay*.

What they had

was like a gentle rain
of seed from the feeder
when finches share

or the confluence
of river joining
from different directions.

Like what you see
when you tilt your head
toward where everything

knows the reason
for which it is designed
or the water stirred

by two children
emerging from where
surf meets sand,

they, kicking their legs
to the sky simply
for the joy
of the world.

First Signs of Spring

The riverbank reveals last year's
crop of rusted cans
and Styrofoam cups once
filled with wax-worms and earth.

Bullying rocks split the creeks
like some bridge troll forcing
recalcitrant water off to the sides.

Soft smells of young
orangewood with creosote
sap laden the bee-filled air.

And off in the distance,
birch-bark dappled with sunlight
like a Monet where footbridge
and pond become one and the same.

How to Write a Poem in a Cafe

There. That woman
with the auburn hair,
down vest. Make up a life
for her. How she fell in love

with the guy from the country
and western band back in
the eighties. A steel guitar
player to be exact. How

she would sit in the back
of the dives and road houses
he played on weekends,
and wrote poems in longhand

that she never showed him
or even later anyone else.
How they fought about
his wanting to use their savings

to go to England to cut a record
that no one would ever buy.
How he left on that weird June
morning when the temperature

almost went down to freezing.
How she dreams now of driving

out to Yellowstone in her beater
of a Buick to see the geysers, feel

the spray on her freckled neck,
sporting a farmer's tan
from painting the siding
on her aged, mother's house.

And how she works the graveyard shift
over at the box factory, comes here
when her time is up, more out
of boredom than anything else,

drinking her third cup of coffee,
black, three sugars, pretending
to work on the Sudoku puzzle
as she invents a life for me.

Love Letter

I have written
        exactly one
perfect poem

in my life
        and it is
for you.

after I am
        gone
you might wish

to read it.
        I keep
it in

the drawer
        of our
nightstand

with my father's
        watch,

a snapshot

of us when we
            were young,
and my upper bridge.

The Woman in Hospice Remembers Paris

She always kept flowers
in the house to paint:
roses, daisies in jade-
green ten-penny
pots, fired and glazed,

like Cezanne, who saw through
the maze of appearance
to the essence, his lemons
luminescent with color
right up to their very end.

Waiting for the Parade

It didn't come yesterday
and the guy in charge
just told me it won't be here
today. He says the morning
must be perfect with just
a hint of trail-high clouds
and the exact, right mixture
of sunlight and shade.
He said that today came close
but in the end, the winds out
of Missouri were just a breath
too strong and the air in Iowa
held the too-great prospect of rain.

Meanwhile, while I was not paying attention,
a foal was born in the pastureland
and my neighbor gave birth to twins.
Five blue-speckled robin eggs appeared
in the aspen outside my window,
the jays in the pines decided
that the family of squatter crows
had to go, and the mid- afternoon sun
warmed my fish pond into a sparrow spa.

And still, I wait, not daring
to budge from this choice,
parade-watching spot here at the curb,

praying for that perfect day yet
to appear, looking to the horizon,
listening as best I can for those first,
promised strains of far-off brass.

Cornflowers

Bachelor Buttons, the old people
called them, found in spring
among rows of corn and winter wheat.

Worn by single men in their lapel,
left buttonhole, if they were available,
right, if they were spoken for.

Today a man plucks one
from the vase on the kitchen table,
picked from the furrows

of his fields He is going into town
to visit his wife of sixty years,
now mute in the nursing home.

He wishes she were here to help him,
his hands are not steady. But he finally
puts it in his button lapel, the right one.

Local Branch

Having your book of poems appear
at the local library branch
is much like being named
Pork Queen in the festival parade.
Like in football when you forward pass
and two of the three possibilities
are bad, the reasons why
your book shows up on the shelf
might be considered suspect.
*He's not selling well
and the least we can do
is help out.* Or:
*He's not that great,
but still and all, he's ours.
Besides, he might draw
a little more traffic
to the 800's stack.
That can't be all bad.*
Anyway, it's patron's comments
that count the most, the consistent
clucking of tongues collected
by the librarian like overdue fines—
*Go figure. And all this time
I thought he was a regular guy.*

Teleology

A thing is good if it fulfills its plan or purpose.

A good letter explains,
he thinks as he writes.
Outside, birds flit and caw,
swooping, defending
their nests against March
and any rival looking
to steal their intended mate.
A good letter explains.
He picks up
the small framed photograph,
a smiling child, a woman peering
out from some other story,
and worries again
if they will understand.

Off the Map

They're pulling out the post office boxes,
the ones with the bronze fronts and inlays of leaves
and single number combination knobs.
They'll all be gone by tomorrow.

Sooner or later the news will leak out
to Rand McNally. The town will disappear
like notes written in invisible ink,
one less place on the map to get through

on the way to where you really mean to go.
East, west, direction makes no difference
when the only way on Main Street
is out. Watch weeds get under the skin

of the pavement while pigeons dance
their two-step that no one will stay around to see.
Old men taking turns on the sidewalk bench
play their parts to empty storefronts hoping

for stage cues that never come, while blackbirds
humming gossip on soon to- be dead
telephone wires, talk in twos and threes,
as if betting on who will be last to leave.

Still Life

The tilt
      of the bowl,
cherries, stems.
      A bread knife
hanging over the table
      edge ready to topple
at a moment's notice.

Late at night,
      he dreams
of what's left
      of a world, silence
his only companion still
      alive and strong
enough to paint the dead.

Somewhere Over Pennsylvania

Sitting under her spotlight beam,
the old lady brings out her cellophane bag
for the fifth time this trip.
She lowers her seat tray taking me
hostage and pulls out her stash.
One by one, she turns snapshots
face up like a casino dealer:
a child riding a tricycle, another
blowing out two candles on a cake,
the third wearing a mask
of spaghetti. She traces

her finger over each like Braille,
then studies a ragged piece of paper,
writing printed in a palsied hand.
They will come, she knows, her daughter
and cold-fish son-in-law to meet her
at the gate with their uncertain
smiles and children. But it never hurts
to have the address, a phone number,
some change handy. After all,
you never know. Far below

the plastic window fogged,
from my cheek, each single farm house
cold and alone as a star struggles
to pull town-light into its orbit.

Coffee, black and oily enough
to lube a tractor sits on a stove,
while porch lights remain on long after
everyone is in for the night for anyone
who might drive down the road
for a visit. After all, you never know.

Mall Walking

The fastest get the inside track
as if making tight turns protects the knees.
Their incandescent sweat suits are bright
and new and their walking shoes squeak
on the tiled floor. Up and back, they cruise
like teens, intent on opening their throttles,
stopping only to count the rpm's that rush
through their necks. They sneak looks
at the clock suspended from the ceiling,
knowing that they must complete their time trials
before being replaced by newer, sleeker versions
in tight Guess jeans or by young mothers
pushing strollers, their arms outstretched
to the finish line. Later, their shoes still warm,
these vintage models will sit, laps full
of the morning paper, sipping coffee
greased with cream, their motors idling.

Open House

The people who live here have left
from two to four to let us poke
about the lives they think will get
us to buy. In the living room, soft
with background music, an art book
rests on the glass coffee table, the warm
smell of basil from the kitchen wafts
so that we might catch the scent
of their happiness. But we see

cabinets with chipped dishes,
burns in the carpet upstairs,
a separated sock its big toe
sneaking out from under
the bed. In the laundry room,
nail notches in feet and inches,
six-month growth spurts stopping
two years ago, not far from the hole
in the wall, no bigger than a knuckle.

So, This is Karaoke

The woman behind the bar
Just lit her fifth Vantage
Of the hour. She rotates
Her hips to the back-beat
As she pours, dances
To the words printing on
The large screen TV
Like some foreign film.

She swirls rum around the rim
Of tall glasses for men
Drunk at the scents
Of old love and beer.
Like bears wandering out

Of winter, they stretch and each
In his turn leans off his stool,
Moves to the mike with a glass
To take his best shot
At filling in the shadows

Of songs. The guy with the gray
Comb-over, clutches the mike
in one hand, a woman
With the other, steering both
To the last patch of empty floor.

He squeezes her to his chest
Like a dream, moving her to his
Rhythm as he sings Willie Nelson
Without having to look
At the words. She closes her eyes,
Feathers her head on his heart,

Lighter than a sparrow, listening
To a song written for her alone;
Dreaming of tonight when
Willie himself will ask
her to accompany him home.

Speed Dating

I'll make this quick.
I get two minutes to make you
think this is not
about me when we know
this is all about me.
One minute to go
to not understate
or overreach, to put
my best foot forward
without sticking it
in my mouth or tripping
over my tongue.
Thirty seconds left
to try to keep you
interested. Just enough
time (perhaps)
to tell you
that the most
important thing
you should know
about me
is

The Safest Town in Indiana

Just 15 crimes per thousand,
the state average is 40.
Of course, if we had a thousand folks
I don't know where we'd put them.
But it's true you know—
most of us are too tired or old
to raise much hell any more.
Crime is for the young
and ours left here long ago.
No, we may not have much
crime but we got plenty
of boredom to spare.
Not much to see except down

this county road, and too far
out in the sticks for cable.
But stay tuned tonight,
because if you know
just where to look,
you just might see
how every blue-lit window
in every darkened house
becomes a screen
where the best dramas
get played out,
and old loves linger
or flicker out without a trace.

The Palm Reader is Packing It In

Since the cops have cracked down
there's no future in fortune telling anymore.
Anyway, she finds it too hard to keep
having to put a good spin
on the cards or make up good news
when the life-lines are all bad.
But it doesn't take a mind reader

to know that the plant is shutting down,
the newspaper is folding and the local
bar-convenience store-video palace
is closing up for good, or how
the downtown is all shuttered
and the store windows littered
with signs for-rent-by-the-week.

Even the pawnshops and cash checking
gyp joints have left the place
to the drunks, the has-beens,
and the plain just-out-of-luck
folks to fend for themselves.
So now this old woman,
her own palms damp

and not quite still, is trying
to predict what will happen
when she calls up her daughter

in Orlando, the one she hasn't spoken
with in two years, and asks
to stay in her basement
until she can figure things out.

She closes her eyes
and tries to imagine the voice
on the other end of the line,
wishes she could tell
in advance how it is all going
to play out, this future, so fragile
it can be crushed by a single word.

Ancestor Trees

West of Thedford, Nebraska

They carried the seedlings with them
from Ohio, Indiana, Wisconsin, Iowa,
in the back of their wagons or as baggage
on milk-run trains. Black ash and green ash,
buckeye, honey locust, linden and maple.
And the conifers: white fir, jack pine,
hill spruce and larch, for windbreaks against
heartaches of black earth that peeled off
from too much wind, not enough rain.
And then they were gone, headed west,

always west, until the census was less than
the square miles of the townships. Farms left
to dry up to sideoak and switchgrass, or pure- purple
cornflowers waiting to burn at first lightning strike.
Only cottonwoods survive, and those
confined to a deserted graveyard, their flowering
catkins wafting seeds to the breeze, roots deep,
drinking in the black brine of a creek, branches
bowing low to the worn, sanded headstones
of loved ones so worn out they had to be left behind.

Fly Over States

From above everything looks
so straight, so square,
lives, land, the separate
half-sections of crops.
From this height
you can't see, can't hear
the low, constant hum

of time flowing, falling like cicadas
that flood the fields with their songs.
Those fields so flat that from above
each moment, each heartbeat
of the people below lasts
so much longer
than anywhere else on earth.

Night approaches.
Tree-breaks, heartbreaks
struggling to protect each single life
from darkening fields
that flicker on then off

by reflected light of fireflies.
Soon autumn will arrive almost
as an afterthought, hawk winds
knife-blade sharp, scything what's left
of prairie grass. All that will

remain the bearded hard-stubble

of corn and the very old
huddling against the inevitability
of snow that blocks whatever sunlight left
to warm sleeping ground and aching bones
of those unwilling or unable to catch
the last red eye to warmer climes.

Pruning a Limb

It always comes as such a surprise
when an oak limb turns dead.
But only last spring we sat under one
of the other full branches and said
how that old limb seemed to produce
less buds, less leaves from year to year,
turning death on itself like gangrene
from branch tip inward to trunk.

We recalled how we planted this tree
with its sister, same size, same day
but how only this one took,
as if determined to survive Midwest
drought, winter cold, and blight,
bound and determined to grow along
with our children who dug the hole,
planted the roots and watered it,
then walked away to live
their own separate lives.

How shocked they would be
if they were here to witness
its ongoing death, to learn all lives
don't play out exactly the same,
that some of us simply are destined to die
in the place where we've been sown.

Bolero Silencio

This samba moon,
    lover of evening
stars, stands

    still, not daring
to take even
    a single step
in any direction.

Such momentary happiness
    cannot end anywhere
except in seasoned

sadness. Sit now,
    wait absolutely quiet
among scattered moonlight.

Even the prismed sky
    cannot keep us
adequate company.
    We must dance

because we have legs,
    love because we have
nowhere left to turn.

My Second Annual Farewell Poem

I think
        I might actually
mean it this time.
Hey, why not
        go out on top,
(although in my case

top is a relative
        term). But then
I think on how
I'd have to
        hermetically seal
my carefully

preserved life
        frozen into boredom.
No, better
to go on risking
        wearing out
my welcome

with you,

      Dear Reader,
trying to redefine
myself with
      every word,
trying to remember

to grow always
      grow
without disappearing
      entirely
from the center.

About the Author

Richard Luftig is a former professor of educational psychology and special education at Miami University in Ohio where he was involved in training teachers of children with disabilities. He is a recipient of the Cincinnati Post-Corbett Foundation Award for Literature and his poetry chapbook as well as one of his short stories were nominated for the Pushcart Prize. His poems have appeared in numerous literary journals in the United States and internationally in Europe, Asia and Australia. Two of his poems appeared in the anthology: <u>Realms of the Mothers: The First Decade of Dos Madres Press.</u> He resides with his wife Diane (who has been nominated for sainthood) in California.

About the Press

Unsolicited Press got its start in 2012 in California and is now based in Portland, Oregon. The press publishes exemplary poetry, fiction, and creative nonfiction from emerging and award-winning writers around the world.

Learn more at www.unsolicitedpress.com.